Standard Grade
GEOGRAPH
REVISION NOT

Richard Goring

Leckie & Leckie

To Ritchie Cunningham for his helpful advice and his assistance as a proof reader.

To Robert Hands and Maggie McHardy for their artwork.

Published by Leckie & Leckie
8 Whitehill Terrace
St. Andrews KY16 8RN
Tel 0334 - 75656

A CIP catalogue record for this book is available from the British Library.

ISBN 0-9515718-2-6

Typesetting & Page Layout by Derek Keiller Advertising Dundee
Printed by Inglis Allen Kirkcaldy

CONTENTS

1. YOUR GEOGRAPHY COURSE

In your third and fourth year geography course, you will cover a wide variety of topics. These are broken down into three main areas, all of which will be tested in your examination.

1. Aspects of PHYSICAL geography, which looks at such things as landforms, the processes which shape the landscapes we see today, weather and climate, how people use the countryside and environmental issues.
2. Aspects of HUMAN geography, which concentrates on settlements, rural changes both at home and abroad, farming, industry and economic change.
3. INTERNATIONAL ISSUES is an area of geography which looks at the differences which populations face across the world. This includes a study of developing countries and the problems which they have to overcome, and the ways in which trade, aid and conflict affect people.

Your final award in geography is made up of three elements. These are:

1. **Knowledge and Understanding** As the name suggests, this tests your understanding of geographical terms and examples. The ability to explain is an important part of this element.
2. **Evaluating** This element tests your ability to reach conclusions, to consider different points of view and to make predictions.

   Both of these elements will be tested in the examination.

3. **Investigating** This element requires you to produce an investigation, of about 10 pages in length, which will be marked by your teacher in the second term of your fourth year. This is not tested in the examination, and suggestions as how to tackle this are found later in this book.

This book of revision notes is designed to help you revise for the examination and produce a worthwhile investigation. Most of the book is concerned with covering the KEY IDEAS of the Standard Grade geography course. It does not tell you everything you need to know for the exam, but it will tell you what you will need to study in order to do your best. Use the book alongside your class notes and any relevant text books you have and use it to direct your study. The next section of the book will give you hints on how to do this effectively.

Finally, you will notice that certain parts of the book are written *in italics*. These are more complicated terms or examples, which may only appear in the Credit paper, so if you are only sitting at General Level, they can safely be ignored.

2. TECHNIQUES OF STUDYING

This part of the book is designed to help you study more effectively. It is divided into three parts:

PREPARATION FOR STUDY
HOW TO STUDY
SOME EXAMPLES

Unfortunately, studying is hard work, although some people find it harder than others. Whilst this book should help you study effectively, it will not do your work for you! Many of the comments and ideas made in this section will be appropriate to your other subjects, too.

PREPARATION FOR STUDY

1. Work out a timetable for each week's study in advance.
2. Leave time within this timetable for any homework you may be given.
3. Don't study every night (or day during the holidays). Take some time off (e.g. Friday and Saturday evenings). This gives you something to look forward to as well as an opportunity to relax and forget your work.
4. Don't feel guilty on your official "time off".
5. Arrange your study time in regular spells, with a break between each spell. (e.g. 6.00 - 7.00, 7.15 - 8.15, 8.30 - 9.30). Try to start your studying as early as possible each evening - while your brain is alert. The longer you postpone working, the more difficult it is to start!
6. Study a different subject for each one-hour spell, except for the day before an exam.
7. During your 15 minute breaks, do something different; have a drink or listen to some music.
8. People study best in silence. No one can study effectively with the radio or TV on. Keep your passion for heavy metal for breaks between study spells.
9. Have your class notes and any textbooks available for your revision as well as plenty of blank paper, a pencil, etc.. It's a good idea to have a jotter for study notes so that you can refer back to them later. Make "Catchword" sheets - they are invaluable, like the example shown below.

CATCHWORD	MEANING
Anticyclone	An area of high pressure
Secondary industry	Industries which manufacture things
Commuters	People who travel into town to work
Erosion	The process of wearing down the landscape

10. Finally, forget all or some of the points in this section if you are happy with your present way of studying. Don't change what is successful!

HOW TO STUDY

There are two main types of revision:

Revision of class notes, worksheets, etc.
Tackling past-paper questions, which can be marked by your teacher.

This book of Revision Notes will help you with both these.

1. When you are revising your class-work, it is no use simply copying them out again (how boring!). Set out the topic under revision and note down all "Catchwords" with a brief description of each. This can best be done on the "Catchwords" sheet. Any points which you think are important should be noted on blank paper, along with any rough copies of maps and diagrams which might be helpful. (Don't spend ages colouring in maps - this is merely timewasting!)

Use this book to break your studying into topics, and to direct your study. Go through each of the pages carefully referring back to your class work-sheets answering any questions which are asked, writing the answers down as you go. You can then refer back to these notes/catchwords sheets at a later date for final revision before the exam.

2. Past-paper questions can be approached in two ways.

a) Under exam conditions, you can set yourself a time for each question and answer it as well as possible without using any references or notes. This will encourage you to answer within the time limit. The length of time for each question depends on the level of paper you are sitting:

for Credit: about 15 minutes per full question;
for General: about 10 minutes;
for Foundation: about 5 minutes.

b) Alternatively, you can answer past-paper questions as if they were an ink exercise, using notes, textbooks etc. to produce a model answer. Your teacher will mark these for you and point out any mistakes.

3. Learning your geography for the exam should not be a case of trying to memorise everything you do in third and fourth year. Much of the course concentrates on case studies or examples (of farms, coalfields, glaciated uplands, cities in the developing world, etc.). In the exam, you will see questions about places you have not studied. Don't panic! You should be able to transfer your knowledge of a topic or theme to a new area. For example, many of the landscape features which are studied in the Scottish Highlands can be transferred to the Scandinavian Highlands, or the Alps, or even the Rocky Mountains in Canada. Economic, social and environmental problems characteristic of declining traditional industries in Lanarkshire are equally true of Northeast England or Northeast France. And so on.

SOME EXAMPLES

Sometimes, of course, it is necessary to learn or memorise facts. There are different ways of doing this, but one way is to use a mnemonic. This is something designed by you to help the memory. Try arranging the first letters of a list into a sentence.

e.g. - Scotland's 5 New Towns:

"**E**very **K**ing **C**an **L**ive **I**n **G**lasgow"

(**E**ast **K**ilbride, **C**umbernauld, **L**ivingston, **I**rvine and **G**lenrothes)

- Scotland's 6 major power stations:

"**L**arge **C**andles **K**ill **I**nsects **T**hrough **H**eat"

(**L**ongannet [coal], **C**ockenzie [coal], **K**incardine [coal], **I**nverkip [oil], **T**orness [nuclear] and **H**unterston [nuclear]).

Can you devise a mnemonic to help you remember the major factors of industrial location (page 28)?

(page 28)

(**R**aw material, **P**ower, **S**ite, **T**ransport, **L**abour, **M**arkets and **G**overnment help)

3. PHYSICAL LANDSCAPES

PROCESSES

1. You should understand that all physical landscapes are shaped by a number of PROCESSES, which act on the landscape and cause it to change. The most important of these processes are EROSION, TRANSPORTATION and DEPOSITION.

2. EROSION is the process which eats away at the landscape, gradually wearing it down. *There are two main types of erosion: PHYSICAL EROSION and CHEMICAL EROSION. Physical erosion occurs when rock is broken up into smaller pieces by the effect of ice, waves, rivers or wind. Chemical erosion occurs when there is a change in the chemical nature of the rock such as when limestone is dissolved by water.*

3. Once rock has been eroded, it is TRANSPORTED away by water, ice or wind.

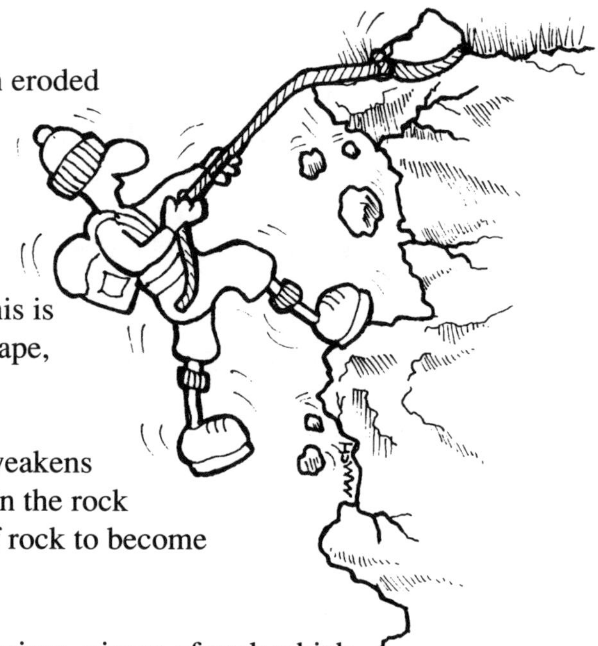

4. Eventually, the material which has been eroded and transported is dumped or DEPOSITED somewhere new. This creates new landforms.

5. WEATHERING is very important, as this is the process which softens up the landscape, making erosion much easier.

   FROST SHATTERING, for example, weakens rock. Water which is caught in cracks in the rock freezes and expands, allowing pieces of rock to become loose.

   Gravity also has a part to play in weathering: pieces of rock which fall off cliffs collect at the foot of the cliff in a SCREE SLOPE. LANDSLIDES are also caused by gravity acting on soil or rocks which are unstable - often the presence of water lubricates the slope and it begins to slide.

6. All these processes act on the landscape over a period of TIME. Sometimes the period of time for change to occur is very short, as in the case of a landslide. Usually, however, the timescale is much longer - in the case of glacial erosion it may be tens of thousands of years.

7. The type of rock *(or GEOLOGY)* in an area is also important in controlling the rate of erosion. Resistant rocks, such as granite, wear down much more slowly than soft rocks, such as chalk. This is why most of the mountains in Britain are composed of resistant rocks; they have resisted erosion more than the softer rocks around them which now form the lowlands.

COASTS AND RIVERS

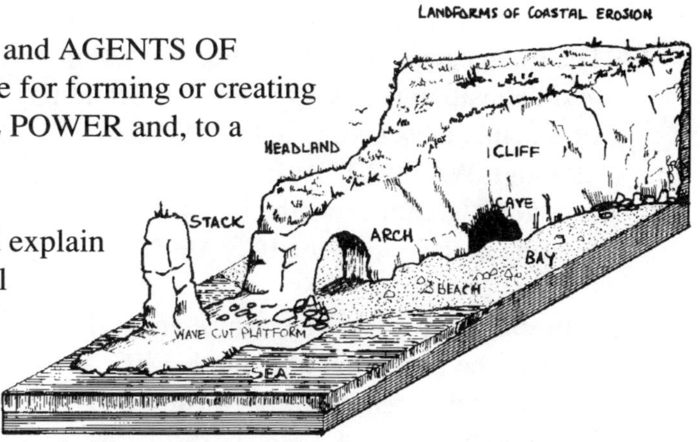

1. The main AGENTS OF EROSION and AGENTS OF DEPOSITION which are responsible for forming or creating coasts are WAVE POWER, TIDAL POWER and, to a lesser degree, WIND POWER.

2. You should be able to recognise and explain the formation of a number of coastal features. These could be features of coastal erosion or coastal deposition. Some of these features are shown in the table below:

LANDFORMS OF COASTAL EROSION	LANDFORMS OF COASTAL DEPOSITION
stack	sandy beach
arch	sand spit
cliff	salt marsh
cave	sand bar
headland and bay	sand dunes
wave-cut platform	

Choose one example from each column above and describe how it was formed, using one or two labelled (or annotated) sketches for each. Be sure to mention which agent(s) of erosion or deposition were involved.

3. The main agent of erosion and deposition which is responsible for creating river landforms is WATER POWER.

4. In the same way as for coastal landforms, you should be able to recognise and explain how the river features in the table below were formed:

LANDFORMS OF RIVER EROSION	LANDFORMS OF RIVER DEPOSITION
V shaped valley	flood plain
gorge	ox-bow lake
waterfall	delta
river cliff (meander)	*slip-off slope (meander)*

Choose any example from each column above and describe how it was formed, using annotated sketches.

5. You should also be aware of the differences in a river in its UPPER, MIDDLE and LOWER COURSES. This refers to the different processes involved at each stage, as well as to the typical landforms and ways that the river is used. This is summarised in the diagram below:

UPPER COURSE	MIDDLE COURSE	LOWER COURSE
mainly erosion mainly erosional landforms upland farming, HEP stations, recreation	erosion and deposition both erosional and depositional landforms small market towns, mixed farming	mainly deposition mainly depositional landforms large towns, ports, large scale industry

GLACIATION

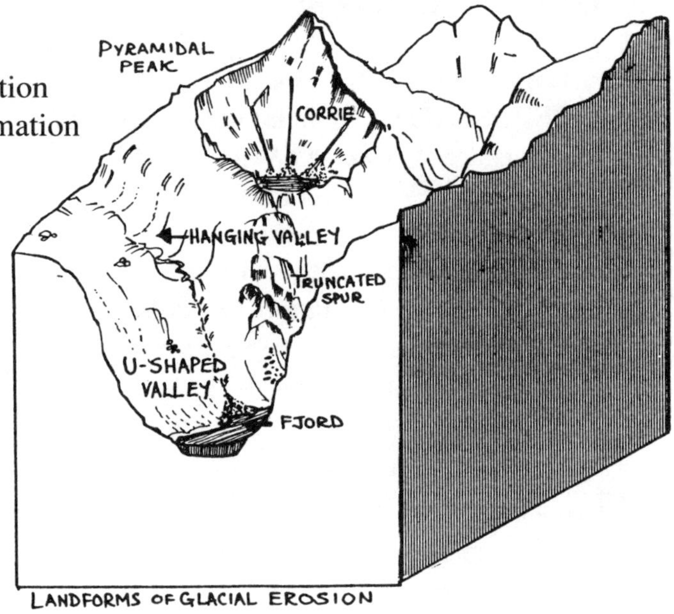

1. The main agents of erosion, transportation and deposition responsible for the formation of glacial landscapes is ICE POWER, although WATER POWER also produced landforms as the ice was melting at the end of the ICE AGE.

2. You should be able to recognise and explain the formation of a number of glacial landforms, including those in the table below.
Choose two examples from each column, and with the help of diagrams, show how each was formed.

LANDFORMS OF GLACIAL EROSION	LANDFORMS OF GLACIAL DEPOSITION
corrie U-shaped valley (and fjord) truncated spur hanging valley arête pyramidal peak (or horn)	till (or boulder clay) end moraine side moraine *esker* *meltwater deposits* *drumlin*

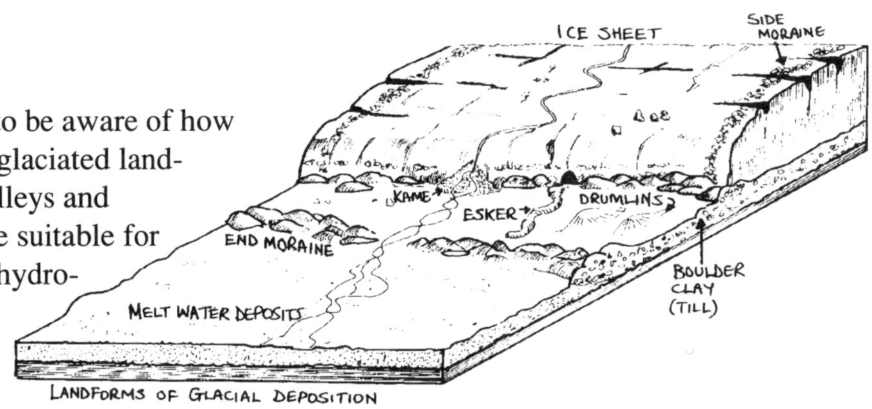

3. It is also important to be aware of how people make use of glaciated landscapes. Hanging valleys and U-shaped valleys are suitable for the development of hydro-electric power; glaciated uplands attract hillwalkers and mountaineers because of their impressive scenery; corries are ideal for skiing; many areas of fertile farmland are found on glacial deposits of till or boulder clay. Other activities to consider include forestry, holiday development, army practice and sand and gravel quarries.

4. THE WATER CYCLE, WATER SUPPLY, STORAGE AND TRANSFER

1. The water, or HYDROLOGICAL CYCLE is an excellent example of a geographical SYSTEM with INPUTS and OUTPUTS.

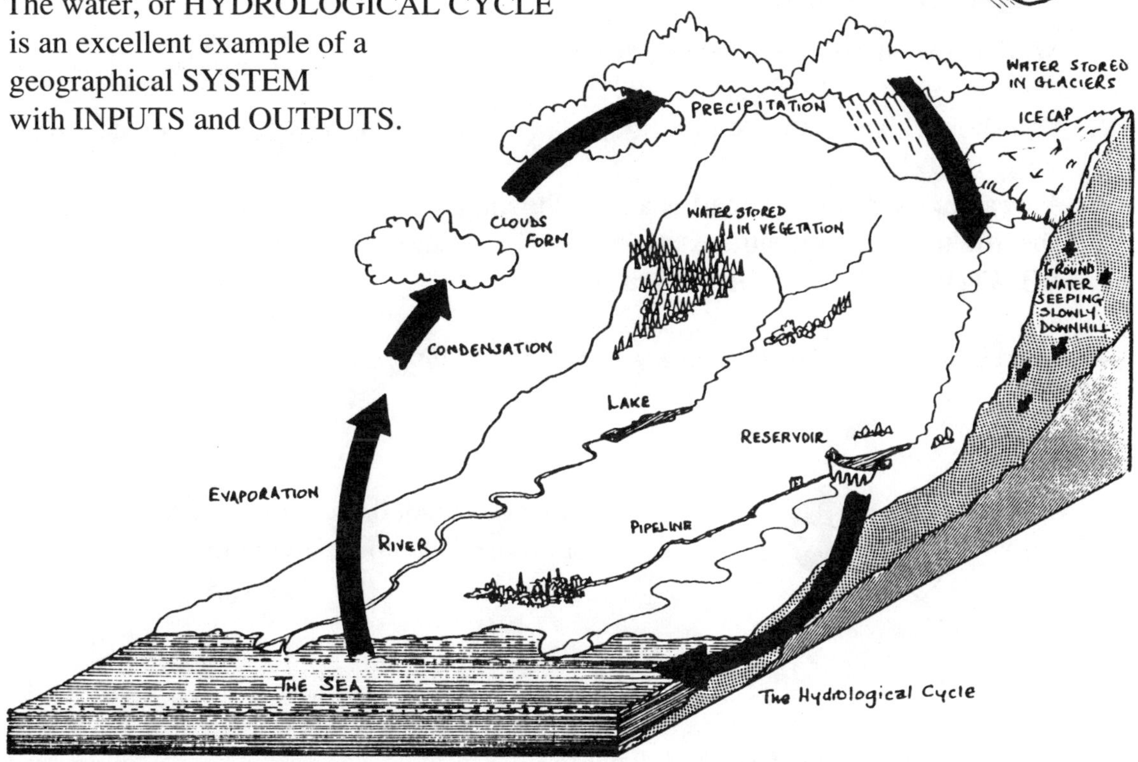

The Hydrological Cycle

2. From the diagram above, you should be able to describe the way in which the hydrological cycle works, with water starting and finishing at the same place.

3. You should also be able to describe how water can be stored, both naturally (e.g. lakes and groundwater) and by human interference (e.g. reservoirs).

4. Water transfer can also take place naturally (e.g. by rivers or seepage) or artificially (e.g. by pipelines to distribute water for domestic or industrial use).

5. Why is it important to move water from one place to another? Areas which use more water than they receive are called areas of water DEFICIT (or shortage). South and East England are good examples of this: rainfall is low, yet population is high, so it is necessary to transport or transfer water from areas which use less water than they receive. Such areas include Wales, Northwest England and most of Scotland: these are areas of water SURPLUS. You should also be able to explain why the west of Britain is an area of high rainfall. Check this out.

6. You should be able to list the inputs and outputs shown in the hydrological cycle diagram above.

5. WEATHER

ELEMENTS OF WEATHER & RECORDING; WEATHER MAPS

1. You should know the main ELEMENTS OF WEATHER. These are: precipitation, temperature, sunshine, wind speed and direction, air pressure, visibility and humidity.

Find out what instrument is used to measure each of these.

What is the unit of measurement of each?

2. You should also be able to describe the layout and position of a weather station.

3. A weather (*or synoptic*) chart is a map showing the actual weather recorded at a specific time. Each weather station's weather is shown on the chart as a WEATHER PLOT or weather symbol.

4. You should know how to read a weather plot like this:

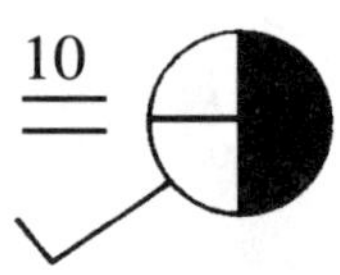

south west wind, 8 -12 knots, mist,
5 oktas of cloud cover, temperature 10°C

5. Weather maps can be described using the following terms:

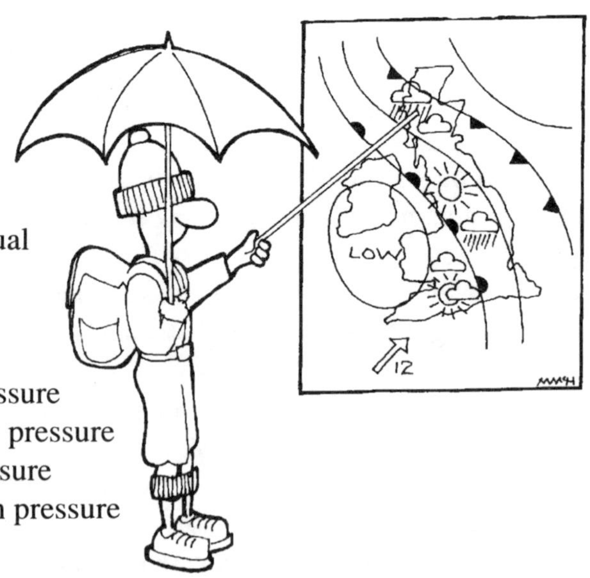

ISOBARS - lines joining points of equal pressure
ANTICYCLONE - an area of high pressure
DEPRESSION - an area of low pressure
RIDGE - a narrow area of high pressure between two areas of low pressure
TROUGH - a narrow area of low pressure between two areas of high pressure

COLD FRONT - a boundary between warm air and cold air
WARM FRONT - a boundary between cold air and warm air
OCCLUDED FRONT - rather like a cold front, this is formed when a cold front catches up with a warm front

WEATHER SYSTEMS, FORECASTING; EFFECTS ON PEOPLE

1. You will also need to know some of the characteristics of anticyclones and depressions. The main features are shown below:

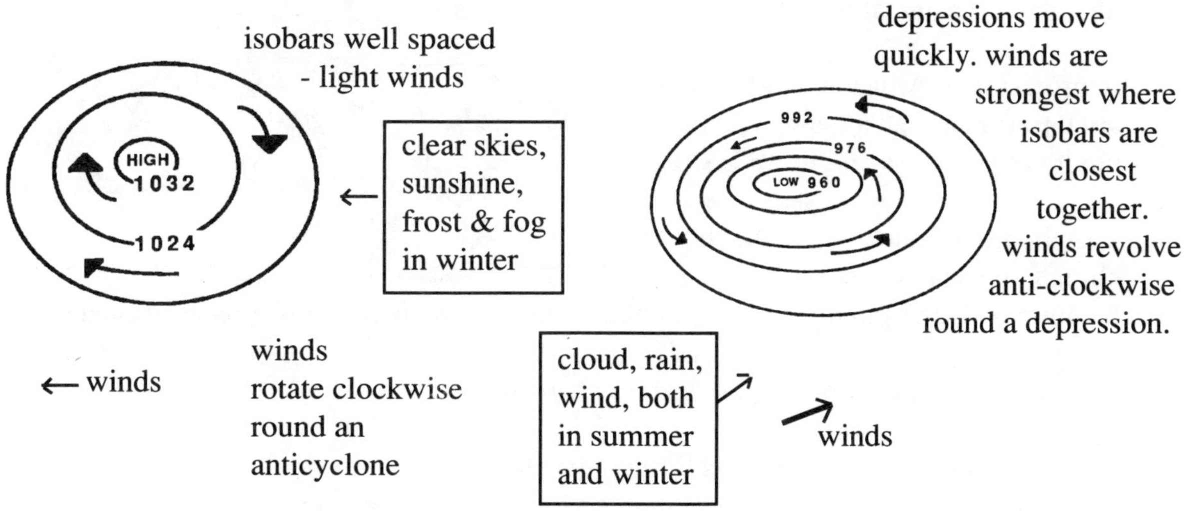

2. When two air masses come together, there is an area of unstable air called a front. You should understand something about the position of fronts through a depression, and how these affect the land they pass over.

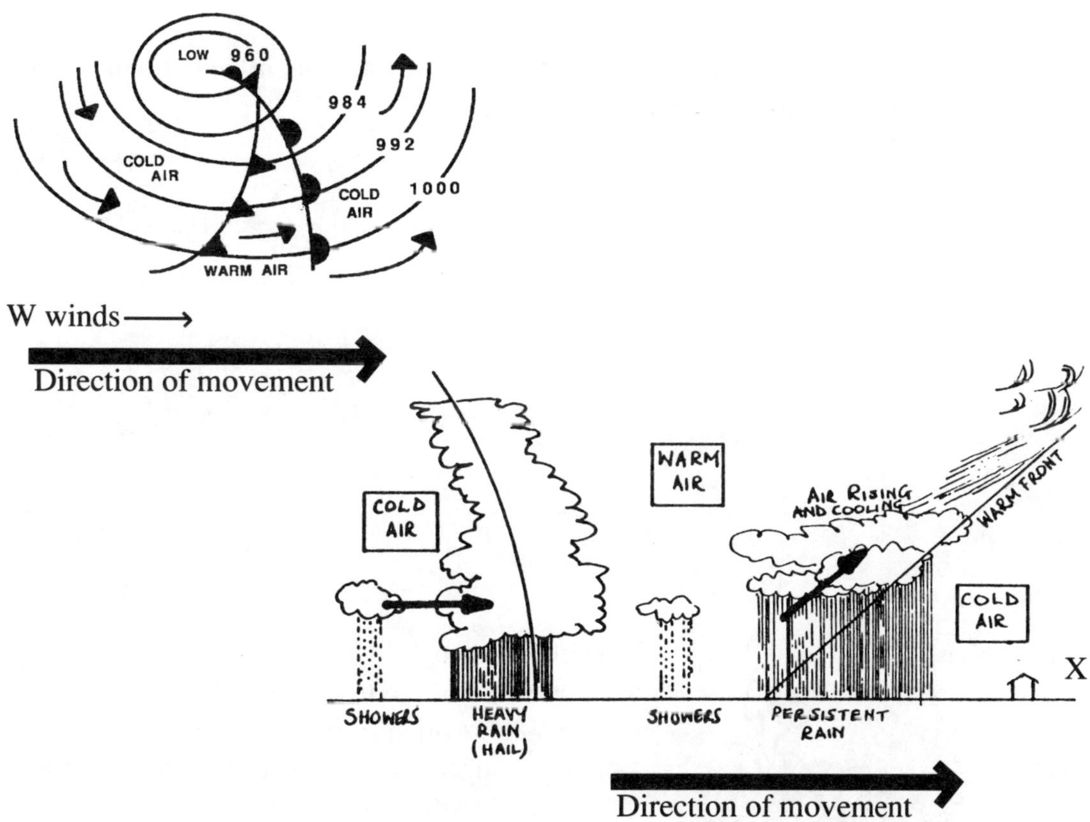

3. Explain what happens to the weather at X in the diagram above, as the depression passes over it. You should be able to refer to wind speed and direction, temperature, cloud cover and precipitation.

6. MAJOR CLIMATIC ZONES

1. Given a world map showing major climatic zones, you should be able to identify and name at least two areas of:

rainforest (e.g. Amazon and Indonesia)
hot desert (e.g. Sahara and Atacama)
tundra (e.g. Alaska and north USSR)

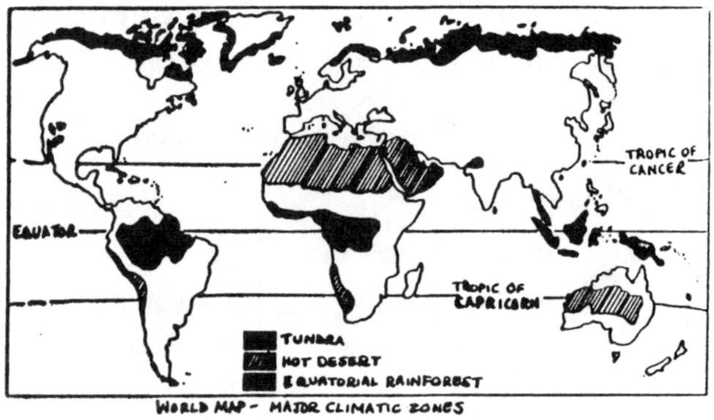

WORLD MAP - MAJOR CLIMATIC ZONES

2. You should be able to describe the climate of each area in terms of temperature and precipitation, and recognise a climate graph which is typical of each area.

3. For each of the areas above, you need to be aware of:

the way in which the climate has limited development. For example, high temperatures and all year round rainfall have made areas of rainforest inhospitable and difficult to live in;

one example of a recent development where, for economic reasons, the difficult conditions have been overcome. This could be oil exploration in the tundra or desert, or mining in the rainforest.

4. You should also be aware of some examples of how such recent developments in such environmentally sensitive areas can have a serious impact on nature.

It would be a good idea to know a little detail about at least one case of environmental damage: possibly the Exxon Valdez oil-spill in Alaska or the cutting down of massive areas of rainforest in the Amazon or Indonesia.
What are the effects of these activities?
How is the damage being tackled?
What lessons have been learned?

5. On a world map, you should be able to identify and name at least one area with:

a Mediterranean type climate (e.g. Italy or California)
a Monsoon type climate (e.g. southeast Asia)

6. Could you recognise either of these from a climate graph showing temperature and precipitation? You should be able to. Use the two graphs below as practice and then describe the typical climate of each.

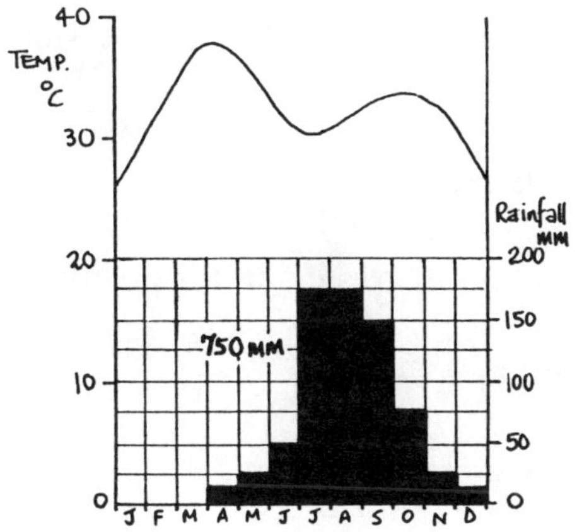

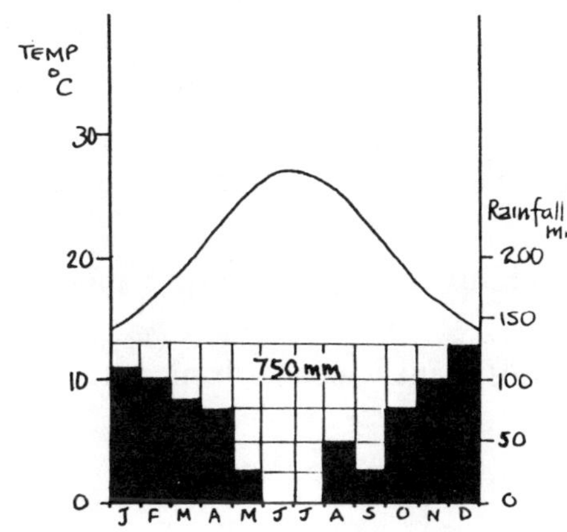

7. You should also be able to describe how each of the climates above has created problems for people living in the area. Places with Mediterranean type climates, for example, suffer from summer drought and high temperatures. Successful agriculture is often only possible using IRRIGATION or water transfer from other areas. Areas with Monsoon type climates often experience torrential rainfall for several months, which can create problems for farming and transport. In both areas, SOIL EROSION can be a major problem. Why can it be a problem?

8. On the other hand, the climates in these areas have advantages too. Many people go to Spain for their holidays. Explain why. And, although farming in Monsoon areas can have problems with too much rainfall, the high temperatures for most of the year mean it is often possible to harvest twice every year - a Godsend for countries which often have large populations.

7. LIMITATIONS ON HUMAN ACTIVITY

1. Over the centuries, people have colonised most of the world's surface. Some areas, such as the tundra, mountains, rainforests and hot deserts, are sparsely populated, because of the hostile climate and environment which make survival difficult.

2. Most of the world's population is found in TEMPERATE and TROPICAL areas, where the climate makes farming easier, and the weather is normally less extreme.

3. As a rule, people choose to live in an area which has:

- a climate that will permit successful agriculture to support the population
- sufficient water to drink and allow crops to grow
- soils which are fertile enough to produce crops and grazing
- land which is flat enough to make transport of people, food and goods easy
- a supply of raw materials (e.g. wood, metals, fuel) which can produce wealth.

Obviously, not all places have all these requirements to the same degree, but it is generally true to say that the better the supply they do have, the more developed that place is. Temperate areas such as Northwest Europe have a good supply of these requirements and so has developed into a wealthy area over the last several hundred years. Less developed areas such as much of Southeast Asia have less of these resources, and it has been difficult to produce wealth and so become more developed.

4. With this century's rapid population growth, which has largely been concentrated in the tropical parts of the world, the pressure on resources has increased. This has meant that there are more people to share what resources there are and so, rather than become more developed as might have been expected, poverty has increased, and many countries are less developed than they were in the past.

8. COMPETITION FOR LAND IN RURAL AREAS

1. In rural areas throughout the world, there are many different ways in which the countryside is used. Farming, mining, forestry and tourism are examples of these different LAND USES. Often different land uses are in competition for the same area of land, and this can lead to conflict. Farmers, for example, can be in conflict with tourists who want access to their land for walking or sightseeing.

2. The diagram below shows some of the land uses which may be in competition with each other.

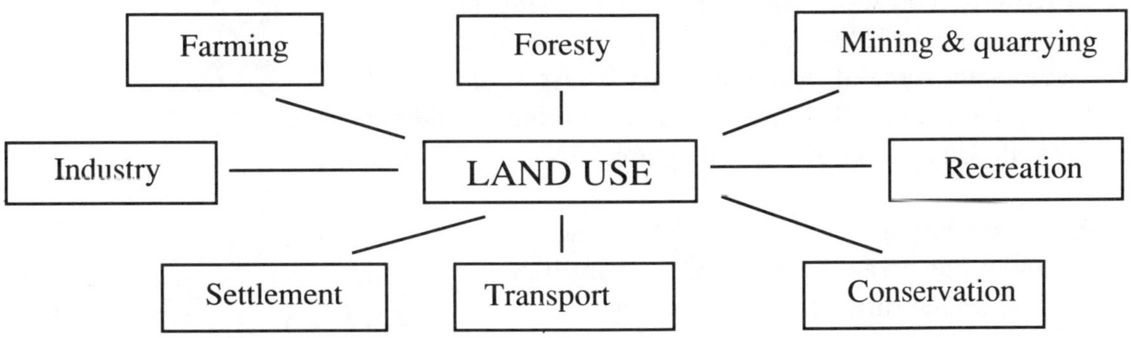

You should be able to describe one actual example of each of the land uses shown above. Recreation could include skiing, climbing, walking, camping, fishing or rallying.

3. It is also important to understand some of the conflicts which may occur. For each of the land use conflicts shown below, you should be able to describe how the demands of each creates problems for the other:

farming v. recreation
mining v. farming
forestry v. farming
industry v. recreation

Can you think of other examples of conflicts? In the exam, you may be asked to give the points of view of both sides in the dispute, for example

for industry v. farming:

"U-shaped valleys in the Scottish Highlands are often ideal for the production of hydroelectric power, because they are easily dammed to give reservoirs and there is high rainfall which allows a steady supply of water. Farmers in the area, however, are against such developments because the land which ends up under water is the lowest and most fertile land in areas where there is very little farmland. Often farmhouses are flooded out and although farmers receive compensation, their future is limited to less profitable hill-sheep farming on the higher land."

CONSERVATION AND URBAN EXPANSION

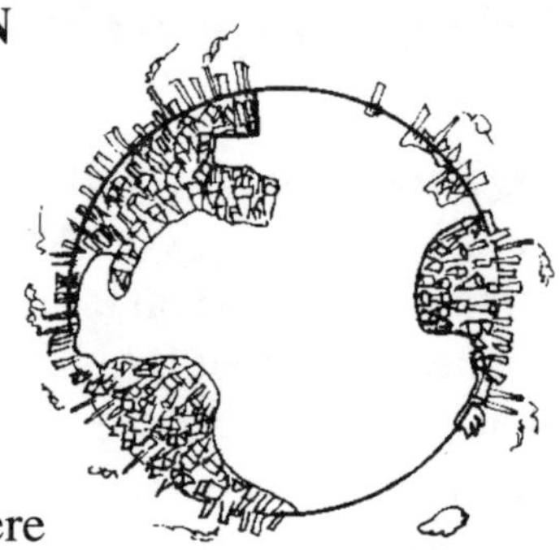

1. As world population grows and cities, particularly in the developing countries, become ever larger, it is inevitable that more and more countryside becomes swallowed up by built-up areas.

2. What makes the problem even worse is that there is a greater urban population requiring land for houses and factories, while at the same time requiring more food from the countryside. And of course, this food is often grown on the land which the cities are expanding into!

3. In the developed world, GREEN BELTS have often been created around cities in an attempt to prevent URBAN SPRAWL. You should be able to name at least one city (e.g. London or Edinburgh) where there is a green belt, and explain some of its implications. These could include higher land values, leapfrogging and breaching. Find out about these if you don't know what they are.

4. In the developing world, pressures on land around urban areas is even greater, as millions flock from the rural areas in search of employment. Poverty and the growth of shanty towns around cities, along with poor health and homelessness make the problems even more difficult to solve. Be able to describe some of these effects in and around a city in the developing world.

5. The main land use pressures around most cities are:

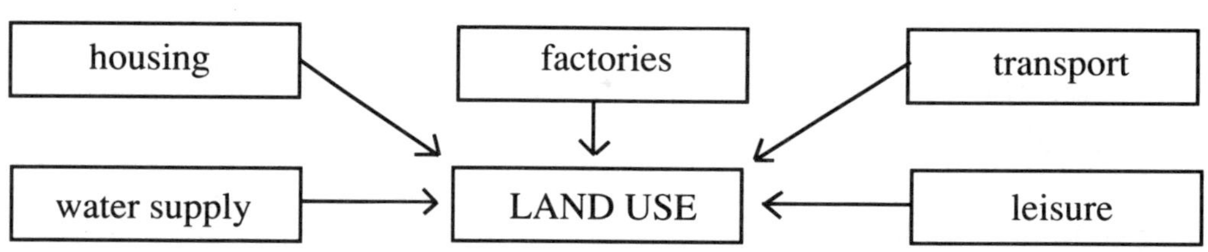

You should be able to explain why each of these exert pressure on the countryside around an urban area.
You should also be able to argue whether the developments of any of these close to an urban area would be a benefit or a problem to that area.

9. RESOURCES

1. Planet Earth can be described as an ECOSYSTEM. This means that it is composed of many millions of living things (plants and animals) which depend on each other for their survival. If there is damage to any of these living things, it will have an effect on others, and there may be far-reaching consequences.

2. There are also many non-living things on Earth. These include RESOURCES such as minerals (e.g. iron and oil), and timber. Some of these resources are RENEWABLE. This means that they will naturally replace themselves if they are given the time to do so. Timber and water power are examples of renewable resources. Other resources are NON-RENEWABLE, and as people use them up, they will become scarcer and eventually run out. Metals and fuels such as coal and oil are examples of non-renewable resources.

3. As the population of the world continues to grow, and people expect an ever-improving standard of living, it is inevitable that resources will be used up at a faster rate. The only solutions that will overcome this problem are to reduce the speed at which we use up resources and attempt to recycle as many resources as possible. Finding alternatives to some scarce resources also helps to reduce the problem.

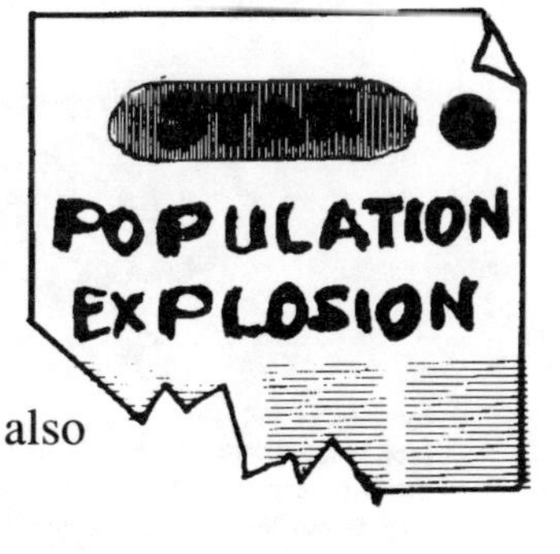

10. CONSERVATION IN SENSITIVE AREAS

In some parts of the world, the impact of resource-gathering is especially damaging.

1. In forest areas, particularly rainforest, the cutting down of forests for timber or farmland has major local implications as well as threatening the global environment. You should be able to describe these effects, and explain the global consequences of forest clearance, tying them in with what is happening elsewhere on Earth. (Greenhouse Effect, Global Warming).

2. In arid (dry) areas, increasing pressure on the land caused by changes in the climate patterns and increasing population leads to land deterioration, and eventual DESERTIFICATION. You need to understand how this process occurs, referring to an area which you have studied. What can be done to reduce this effect?

3. Oceans have also suffered greatly in the last 100 years from the dumping of waste, over-fishing and pollution. You should be able to describe how oceans are so vulnerable, using an example such as over-fishing in the North Sea or oil-spillage (e.g. Alaska).

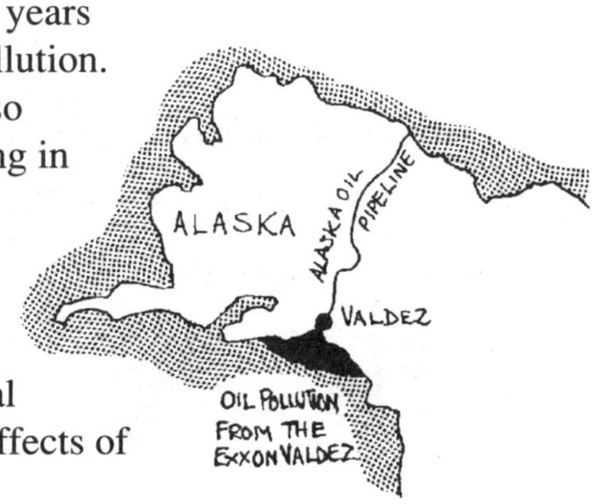

You should be able to explain why forests, deserts and oceans are so liable to be damaged. This means you will have to think about the local ecosystems, local people, as well as the global effects of damage.

In other words, why is conservation of these areas so important?

FOREST CLEARANCE CAUSES FLOOD DISASTERS IN LOW LYING BANGLADESH

11. SETTLEMENTS WHAT IS A SETTLEMENT?

1. A SETTLEMENT is a place where people live and work. The size of a settlement can vary from a single building (e.g. a farm) to a major city such as London with around 7 million inhabitants.

2. Depending on their size, settlements are often described as:
   HAMLETS→VILLAGES→TOWNS→CITIES→*CONURBATIONS*
   (smallest) (largest)
   Can you name examples of each of the above?

3. There are many more small settlements than there are large ones. Can you explain why?

4. There are many different LAND USES to be found in settlements. These include:

RESIDENTIAL	(housing)
COMMERCIAL	(shops and offices)
INDUSTRIAL	(factories)
RECREATIONAL	(parks, sports facilities, etc.)
WASTE LAND	(derelict buildings, cleared land)
TRANSPORT	(roads, railways)

   You should be able to identify these on an Ordnance Survey map.

5. Very often, the different land uses listed above are found in certain parts of a settlement. The shops and offices are usually to be found near the centre of the settlement. In large towns and cities, this commercial area is usually called the CENTRAL BUSINESS DISTRICT (or CBD).

6. In larger towns and cities, it is often possible to see a clear pattern of land use which reflects the development of the settlement. The distribution of urban land use can be explained using one of the following MODELS OF URBAN LAND USE:

1 CONCENTRIC RINGS MODEL, where the city has grown outwards from its old centre

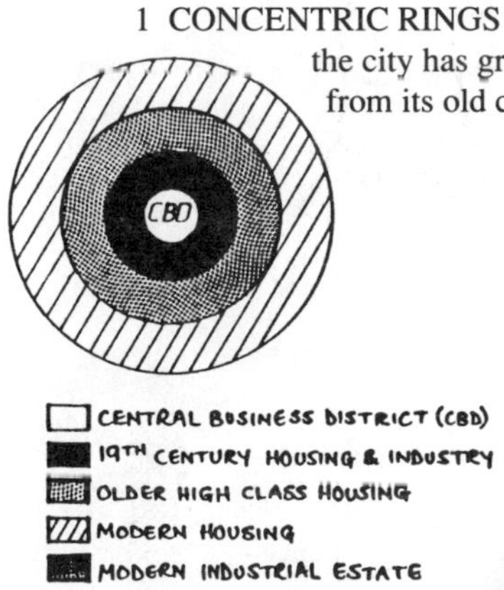

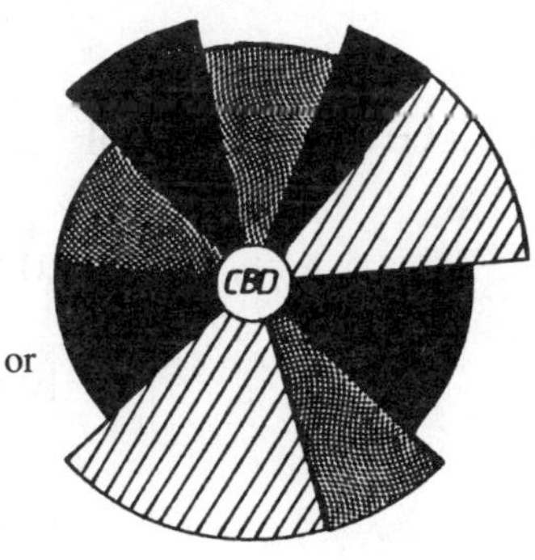

2 SECTOR MODEL, where the city has grown around transport lines such as canals or railway lines

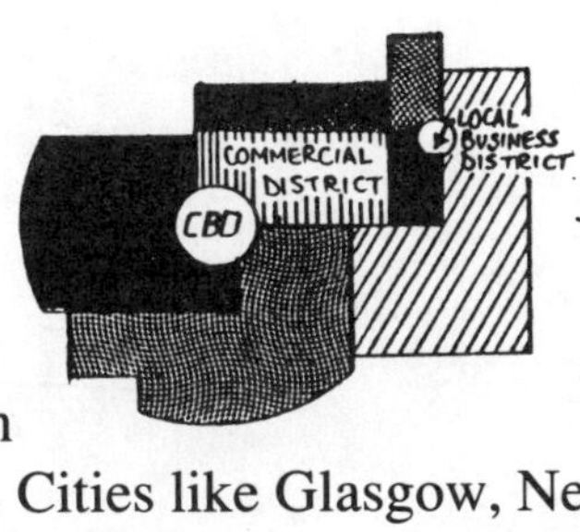

3 MULTIPLE NUCLEI MODEL, where the city has grown around more than one centre (or CBD).

Check this out using an Ordnance Survey map. Cities like Glasgow, Newcastle, Leeds, and Manchester are good examples. You should be able to decide which of the models above can be used to explain the city's development.

SITE, SITUATION AND FUNCTION

1. The initial location of a settlement is influenced by its SITE.

2. The site of a settlement is the area of land on which it is built.

3. The original site of a settlement may have been chosen for a number of reasons, for example:

- on a hill for defence
- on dry land above marsh

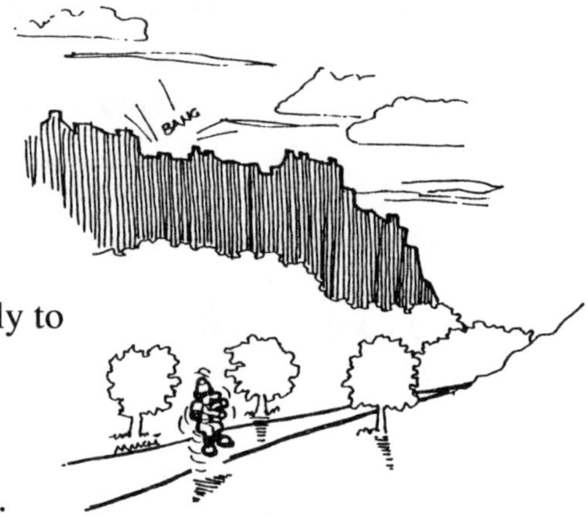

Describe the SITE of the settlement where you live.

4. Even if the site of a settlement is excellent, it is unlikely to grow into a large town or city unless it has a good SITUATION.

5. The situation of a settlement relates to its whereabouts. This is influenced by good routeways, access to a harbour or a raw material such as coal.

Describe the SITUATION of the settlement where you live.

6. Each settlement has a definite character of its own. This is largely due to its FUNCTION.

7. Examples of the function of settlements include:

- market town
- holiday resort
- port
- mining town
- administrative centre
- manufacturing town

Give one example of each type of settlement listed above

a) in Scotland

b) in England or Wales

c) in Europe

SERVICES AND SPHERES OF INFLUENCE

1. Settlements provide SERVICES to those who live or work in them.

The bigger the settlement, the more services it usually provides. A village, for example, might only have a small shop and post office, a telephone box, a public house and an hourly bus service to the nearest town. These can be described as LOW ORDER SERVICES.

A large town, on the other hand, will have many services. Not only will it have many more shops and bus services, it will have specialised services like department stores, record shops and cinemas. Services such as these are called HIGH ORDER SERVICES. They rely on custom from a large population in order to be profitable, so they are only found in towns or cities. You should be able to think of examples of low order and high order services in your local area.

2. Services attract people who want to use them from the surrounding area. This area is called the SPHERE OF INFLUENCE of that particular service.

A low order service, such as a newsagent, will only attract people from close by, so it has a small sphere of influence.

A high order service will have a larger sphere of influence, as people are prepared to travel further to use it. A good example of this is Hampden Park, which attracts football fans from all over Scotland to watch an important international match.

3. The diagram below shows the spheres of influence of two different services: a village store and a large supermarket in a town.

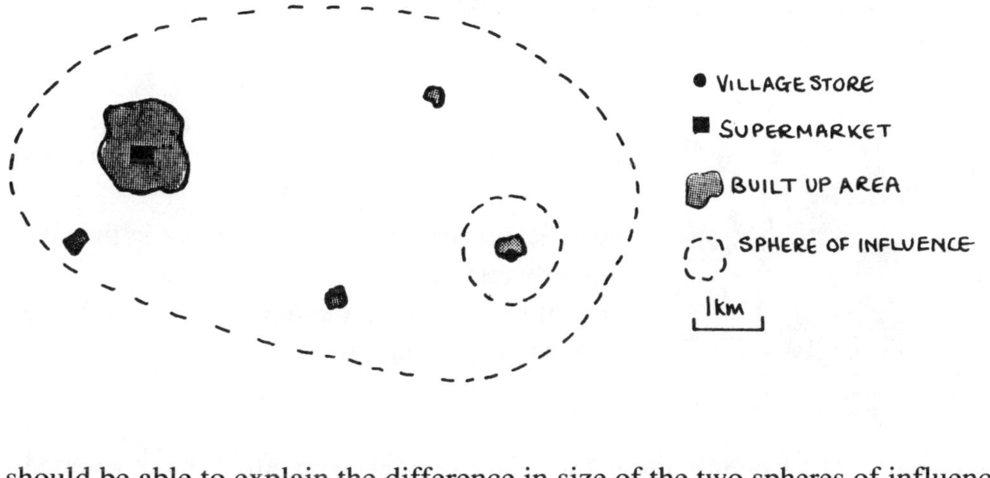

You should be able to explain the difference in size of the two spheres of influence.

12. URBAN GROWTH AND CHANGE

THE PROBLEMS OF URBAN GROWTH

1. The population of the world continues to grow, and more and more people decide to live in urban areas, as this is where the jobs are.

As urban areas grow larger, there are often problems. Pollution, congestion, overcrowding and stretching of resources like water supply or sewage disposal are examples. Cities in DEVELOPED COUNTRIES and cities in DEVELOPING COUNTRIES have different problems.

2. In developed countries, such as Britain, cities such as London grew in size through much of the 19th and 20th centuries. The rapid growth was largely due to developing industries, ports and the expansion of business.

3. This has often led to urban problems which include:

- poor quality housing (e.g. TENEMENTS)
- URBAN SPRAWL with SUBURBAN GROWTH
- greater travel distance to work
- lack of car parking space, inadequate public transport and building of urban motorways and ring roads
- traffic CONGESTION and pollution
- loss of jobs in traditional industries and docks, leading to urban dereliction and waste ground.

You should understand how each of the problems mentioned above has come about, and also how it has affected one city you have studied.

4. In developing countries, such as India or Brazil, the sudden growth in city size has been particularly obvious in the last 40 years. Rapidly increasing rural population has led to MIGRATION from the countryside to the towns and cities.

5. The problems of cities in developing countries are therefore rather different to those in developed countries:

- overcrowding, with many people living in sub-standard housing. This may include SHANTY TOWNS, often built on the very edge of the city.
- insufficient work for those who live in the city
- poverty and disease
- lack of services (e.g. medicine) and food for the ever expanding population

6. In the early 20th Century, the world's largest cities were all in the developed countries; now the vast majority are in the developing countries. You should be able to describe the problems found in some detail, referring to a city you have studied.

URBAN CHANGE

1. The problems of urban growth described on page 24 have been tackled in many different ways, some more successful than others.

2. Cities in developed countries (such as Britain) have

- knocked down many of the old buildings near the city centres and replaced them with multi-storey flats
- built large housing estates at the edge of the cities, to accommodate people who used to live in old housing
- built NEW TOWNS some distance from the city with the attraction of new jobs and more pleasant surroundings
- renovated many of the old buildings which were structurally sound but lacked modern facilities
- created new areas of housing on the sites of old factories, often near the city centre or docks.

You should he aware of the advantages and disadvantages of each of the solutions above, in terms of:

the SOCIAL aspects (on family and friends, travel)
the ECONOMIC aspects (employment, shopping)
the ENVIRONMENTAL aspects (attractiveness of changes)

3. Cities in developing countries have very different problems:

- how to improve the quality of life for those living in shanty towns
- how to slow down the rate of migration to the cities.

You should be able to describe how one city you have studied has tried to overcome some of its problems.

13. FARMING

FARMING SYSTEMS

1. Any farm can be thought of as a SYSTEM, with inputs, processes and outputs. This is true of farms in any part of the world.

2. Farming can also be thought of as a cycle, which usually takes a year to complete.

   The diagram below shows a very simple farming cycle:

   Farmer → plants seeds → rain falls → harvests crop → sells crop at market → money → Farmer

   Can you identify 2 inputs and 2 outputs in the farming system above?

3. In real life, farming systems are usually much more complicated. There are many different kinds of INPUTS which might include:

TYPES OF INPUT	EXAMPLES
Physical inputs	soil, rainfall, sunshine, altitude
Human inputs: economic	profitability, rent, transport costs
technological	machinery, fertilisers, pesticides
social	labour, demand
political	government SUBSIDIES

4. There are also many different PROCESSES taking place on a farm. Just which processes depend on the type of farm, but examples might include planting, grazing, milking and harvesting.

5. In the same way, the OUTPUTS from a farm will vary: they might include the crop grown on the farm, milk, calves, wool and, if the farm is profitable, money. In poorer countries, where farmers only grow enough food for themselves and their family, money is seldom an output. Farms like this are called SUBSISTENCE farms.

6. It is important to realise that the farmer is a DECISION MAKER. The decisions he makes will affect his profitability. A British farmer will have many more choices available to him than to a farmer in a country like Ethiopia. You should be aware of the kinds of decision a farmer has to make, and the consequences of such decisions.

DIFFERENT TYPES OF FARM

1. Although you may study farming processes on different types of farms, the only types of farms you will have to know about for the exam are ARABLE and PASTORAL farms. Some farms may combine both of these, of course (MIXED FARMS).

2. Arable farms produce crops. You should have some idea of the types of inputs and outputs for an arable farm, along with some of the processes which take place on the farm. In the exam, you may be faced with a question about a type of arable farming which you have never studied in an area you know little about. Don't panic! You will not need to know any details about the crops produced or the local area. If you do need to know anything, then the relevant information will be given to you in the question. What you know about arable farming from your course will let you answer the question. This would include such things as:

   - why are arable farms usually found in dry, warmer areas?
   - what have been the main changes in farming processes in recent years? (e.g. removal of hedges, greater use of machinery, larger farms produced by AMALGAMATION, the importance of European Community subsidies and policies)

3. Pastoral (or LIVESTOCK) farms rear animals, for their meat and for their produce (e.g. milk or wool). Once again, you should know something about the inputs, processes and outputs from pastoral farms. You should be able to describe:

   - why pastoral farms are normally found in higher, wetter or colder areas than arable farms
   - what the main problems are facing today's pastoral farmers
   - what the changes are which have come about in recent years.

4. There are also a number of issues which affect all farmers. Make sure you can describe:

   - why there is concern about INTENSIVE farming methods
   - what effects recent changes have had on the environment (e.g. the greater use of fertilisers and pesticides, the introduction of 'SET ASIDE' land)
   - how farmers are coping with these changes.

14. INDUSTRY

CLASSIFICATION

1. Industry can be classified as PRIMARY, SECONDARY, TERTIARY *(or QUATERNARY)*.

Give 3 examples of each of the above.

2. Secondary (manufacturing) industry can also be described as LIGHT or HEAVY INDUSTRY. Know at least 3 examples of each.

3. INDUSTRIAL LOCATION is dependent on a number of factors. These include:

PHYSICAL FACTORS	HUMAN FACTORS
raw materials	labour requirements
power	markets
site	capital
transport	government policies
climate	

For a large industry in Scotland, consider which factors of industrial location were important in its choice of location (e.g. IBM Computers at Greenock, Torness Nuclear Power Station, Caledonian Paper at Irvine, BP Grangemouth Oil Refinery).

4. Industry undergoes change through time.

a) Many industries have CLOSED DOWN because they were inefficient, too far from modern markets, or their product was no longer in demand. These are often described as TRADITIONAL INDUSTRIES or SUNSET INDUSTRIES.

b) Other industries RELOCATED, because their source of raw materials changed and/or their markets changed.

c) Some industries have undergone REHABILITATION to meet the requirements of modern demand. This has involved modernising buildings and/or updating machinery.

d) The most recent development in industry has been the dramatic growth of HIGH TECHNOLOGY INDUSTRIES which specialise in micro-electronics. Sometimes these are called SUNRISE INDUSTRIES.

INDUSTRIAL CHANGE

1. The location of industry and the importance of different industries changes over time.

2. PRIMARY INDUSTRY: As raw materials become exhausted or cheaper sources become available, mines close down. Over-fishing in certain areas and changes in the demand for farm produce also cause changes in the location of industry.

   You should be able to describe the decline of an industry you have studied in a particular area. One good example is coal mining in Central Scotland.

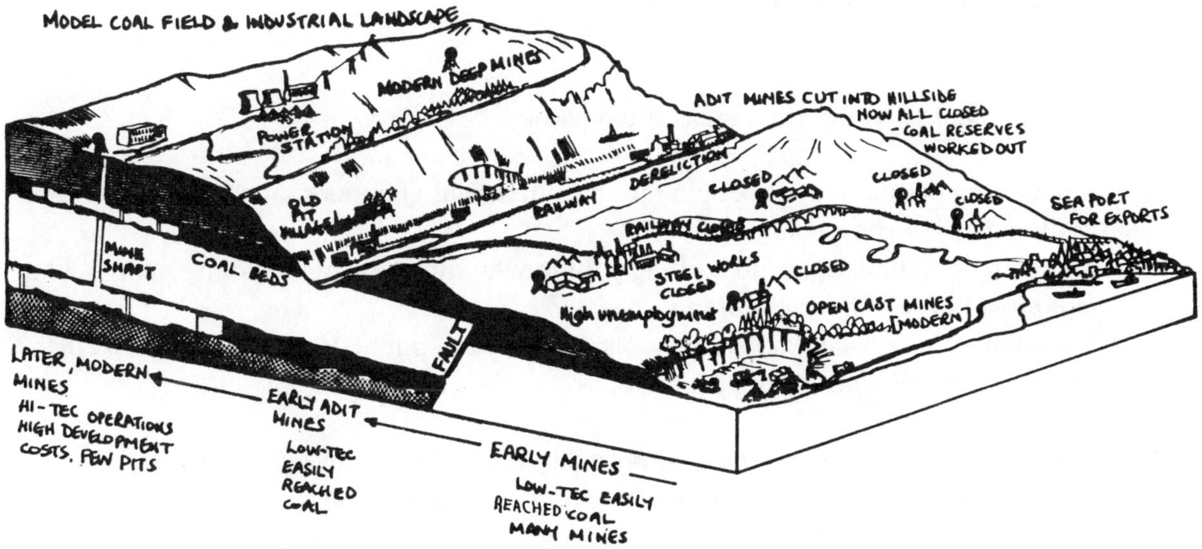

3. SECONDARY INDUSTRY: As the source of raw materials changes, the demand for products changes, or factories become out-dated, the location of manufacturing industry also changes.

   You should be able to describe why a particular industry is no longer important in a certain area. Examples could include shipbuilding on the Clyde or steel-making in Lanarkshire.

4. TERTIARY INDUSTRY: The more developed a country becomes, the more people work in service industries.

   Can you explain the growth of a service industry over the past 20 years? Examples might be tourism in Scotland, stock-broking in the City of London, or health and education in a developing country.

5. When traditional industries close down, they often have a severe impact on the local area. You should be aware of the social, economic and environmental effects of industrial decline on an area you have studied. You might be able to think of benefits too, such as reduced pollution or fewer ugly scars on the landscape.

15. POPULATION

POPULATION STRUCTURE IN RURAL AREAS

1. The population of an area depends on:

- the rate of natural increase. In other words, how many babies are born (BIRTH RATE) and how many people are dying (DEATH RATE).
- the rate of MIGRATION into or out of the area.

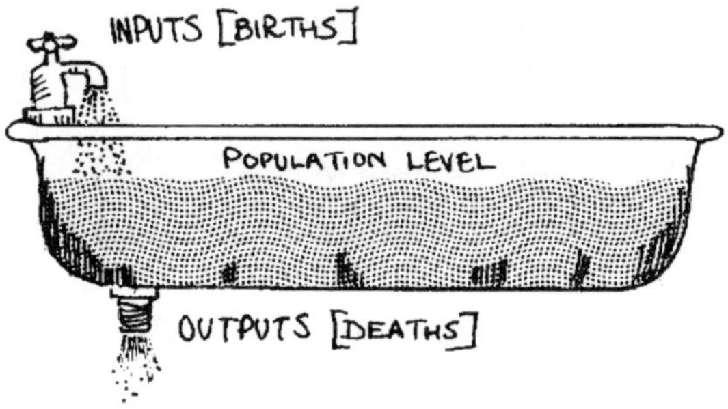

2. In the developed world, rural areas often show

- a declining population, as people move from a relatively poor area to wealthier areas with better job prospects
- an ageing population, as most of the people who move away are young people who are most likely to have children
- a reduction in services such as schools, health care, public transport, shops, as there are fewer people left to support them.

3. In the developing world, the problems are similar but much more noticeable. Migration from rural areas is often very great because of

- rapid population growth which means too many mouths to feed and not enough food

- increasing poverty and starvation

-the chance of work and better living conditions in the cities.

4. It is worth noticing, however, that in some areas, people are being attracted back to the rural areas. In Scotland, for example, towns like Aviemore and Invergordon have encouraged people to move there because of the development of manufacturing or tourist industries. Often this is heavily supported by Government grants in attempt to reduce rural depopulation.

You should be able to explain why there is a decline in the number of services in rural areas in an area such as rural Wales.

MIGRATION: PUSH AND PULL FACTORS

1. Rural migration is usually explained by

   - PUSH FACTORS (which force people to move away), and
   - PULL FACTORS (which attract people to cities).

2. You should be able to describe the push and pull factors which operate in developed countries as well as in developing countries.

3. People who move are called MIGRANTS. There may be social, economic or political reasons for moving from rural areas. Can you give at least one example of each for

   - a developed world area
   - a developing world area?

4. When people are forced to move and leave everything behind, they are called REFUGEES. You should be able to describe one example of this - it might be for political reasons such as war, or economic reasons such as famine.

5. You should also know why cities in the developing world are growing much faster than cities in the developed world.

   Why were most of the largest cities in the world 50 years ago in the developed world, whereas today the largest cities are in the developing world?

   You should know some detail about the effects of migration on

   - a rural area in the developed world (e.g. rural Wales)
   - a developing world city (e.g. Mexico City or Calcutta)

DISTRIBUTION OF WORLD POPULATION

1. World population is very unevenly distributed. In order to explain this, it is often of more value to think about POPULATION DENSITY rather than the total population of a country or region. Population density is described as the number of people per square kilometre.

You should be able to look at a map showing world population density and explain why some areas are densely populated while others are not. This could be due to

- environmental reasons (e.g. climate or altitude)
- economic reasons (e.g. good farmland or natural resources)
- political reasons (e.g. war).

2. As explained on page 30 , the rate at which population changes depends on the relationship between BIRTH and DEATH RATES. If the birth rate is greater than the death rate, population increases. This can be shown in a graph, which can be divided into three phases.

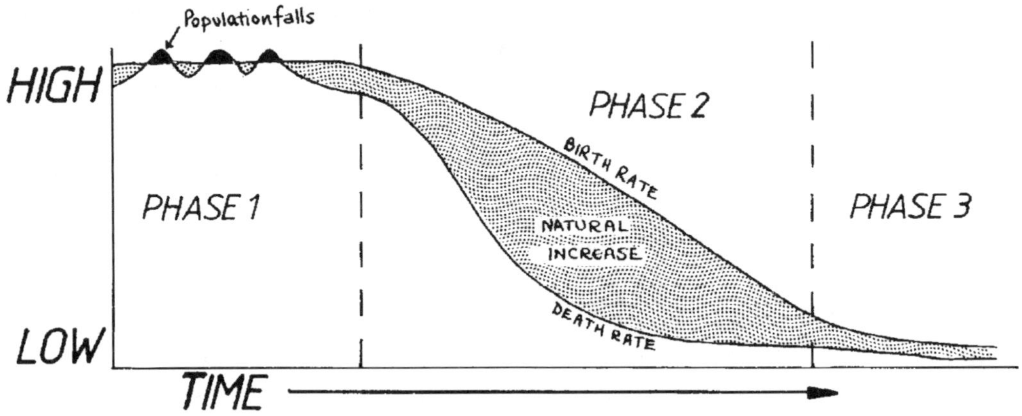

You should be able to state what is happening to the total population in a country in each of the three phases, and explain why birth and death rates change over time. In phase 1, why are both birth and death rates high? What might cause death rate to rise above birth rate? In phase 2, why does death rate fall rapidly, while the reduction in birth rate take much longer? In phase 3, why are both birth and death rates so low? You should also be able to give examples of countries at each phase of the graph.

3. Population details are gathered in each country by a CENSUS. In many countries, this is not very accurate. This may be because the people completing the details may not be very literate, or people in an area may be so spread out that they can be missed. Sometimes, it is possible to avoid paying taxes or fighting in a war by not being included in the census!

POPULATION PYRAMIDS AND LEVELS OF DEVELOPMENT

1. Population pyramids are a useful way of comparing the population of different countries.

You should be able to recognise the shape of a pyramid which represents:

- a developing country

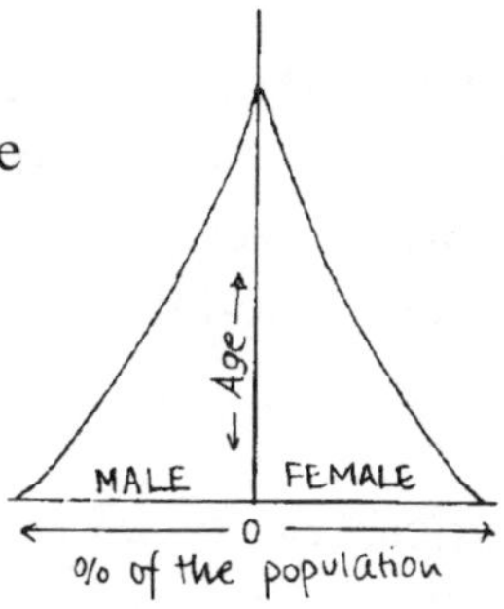

- a developed country

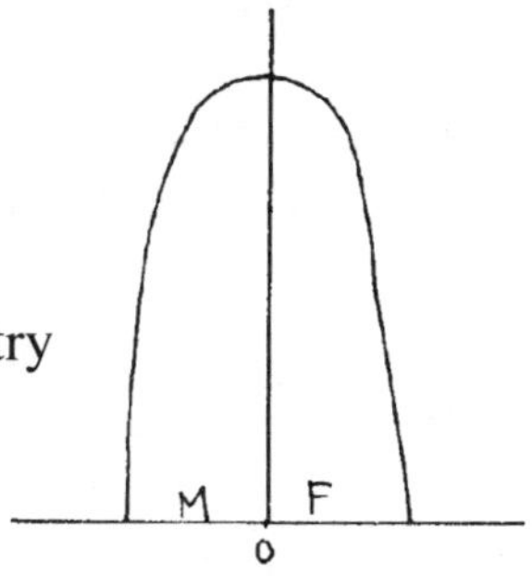

- *a country which has a large number of immigrant workers*

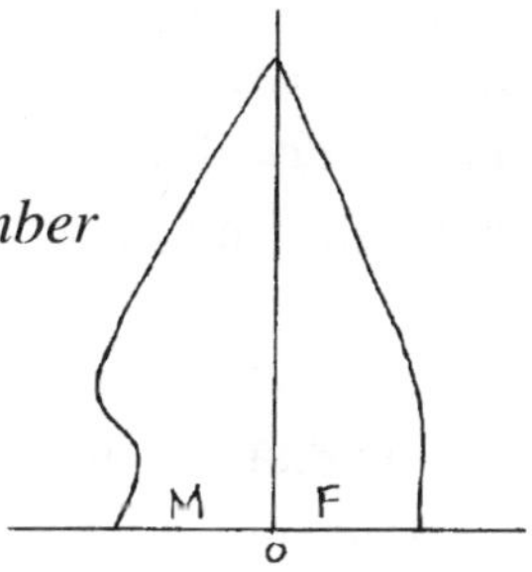

- *a country which has suffered a disaster such as famine or war*

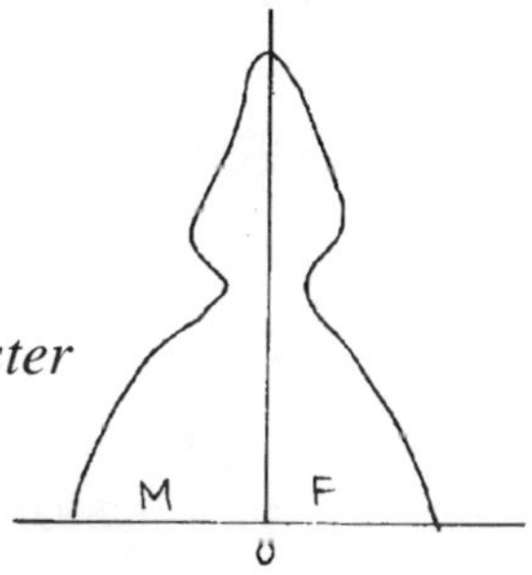

2. It is also possible to compare developing and developed countries by looking at a number of social and economic factors.

The table below shows the differences you would expect to find in some of these factors, but remember there are many others which could be used:

MEASURE OF DEVELOPMENT	DEVELOPING COUNTRY	DEVELOPED COUNTRY
% literacy	low	high
% working on farms	high	low
% population under 15 years	high	low
% population over 64 years	low	high
hospital beds per 1000 people	low	high
car ownership	low	high
Gross National Product (GNP)	low	high
population growth	fast	slow
Life Expectancy	low	high

16. TRADE AND INTERDEPENDENCE

1. No country in the world is entirely self-sufficient. In order to buy in things which it needs from other countries (IMPORTS), it has to sell to other countries things which it produces itself (EXPORTS). The difference in value between imports and exports is called the BALANCE OF TRADE.

Obviously not all countries can sell more than they make, so some countries have a trading SURPLUS (or profit), while others have a trading DEFICIT (or loss).

2. The countries which developed earliest (such as those in Western Europe and North America) did so because they were able to turn raw materials into manufactured products which were then sold to produce wealth. Many of these raw materials came from their COLONIES.

3. Many developing countries, which were often former colonies, are still the main producers of raw materials, which they export to the developed countries. Unfortunately for them, the price they are paid for the raw material is only a fraction of the value of the item it is made into. Often they have to import that item from the developed world. In many cases the gap between rich and poor countries continues to increase.

4. What makes things even worse is that the price paid for the raw material is often controlled by the developed countries.

5. How can this situation change to the advantage of the developing countries? How can developing countries make more money from their raw materials? Who provides the money for industrial development in developing countries?

You should be able to explain how a country can become trapped in its dependence on another country, and describe some of the ways in which this dependence can be broken.

Examples might include timber from the rainforests of Brazil, copper from Zambia, or oil from Nigeria.

6. Many of the developing countries make most of their money by selling exports to the developed countries of the world. Very often, a very large part of their income is from the sale of only one raw material. This makes them very vulnerable to variations in the price paid for that item. Zambia, for example receives over 95% of its export income from the sale of copper.

You should be able to describe the effects that a drop or rise in the price of copper would have on Zambia. This would include employment, earnings, standard of living, investment in industry, education and health, and pressure on the government.

The answers you make could refer to any other developing country, which relies heavily on the export of one product.

7. The prices of manufactured goods have risen far faster than the prices for raw materials. As suggested on page 34 developing countries import mainly manufactured goods, so the money they make from their exports doesn't go as far as it once did. One way of overcoming this problem is to enter into a COUNTERTRADE agreement. Instead of receiving money for exports, the developing countries receive goods. More and more countries are trading in this way.

Try to find an example of a countertrade agreement, and, in your own words, explain why it helps the developing country.

17. DIFFERENT TYPES OF AID

1. Many of the developed countries give aid to the developing countries to try to improve their standard of living. This aid takes many forms, as shown in the diagram below:

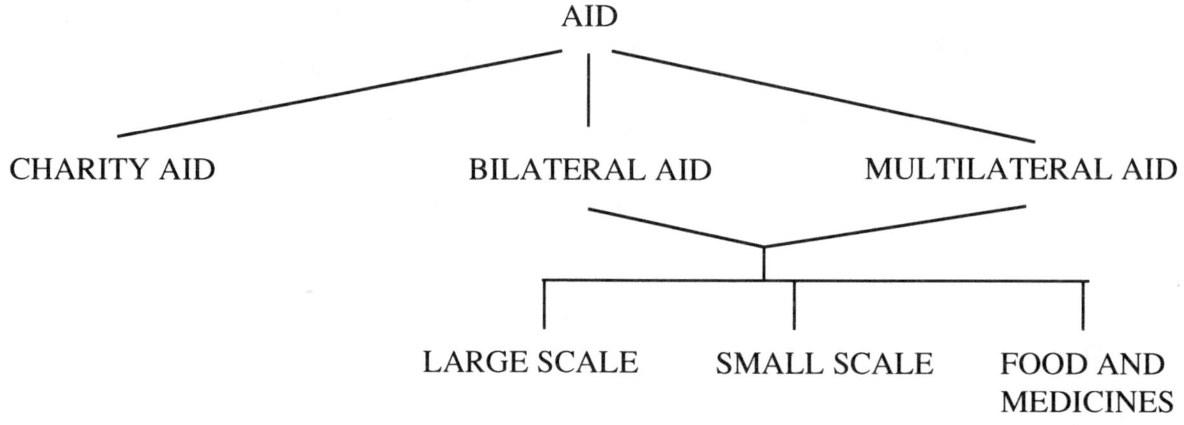

2. CHARITY AID is collected in many countries and used to finance small scale schemes such as improving water supply, educating farmers in new techniques and providing irrigation. At times of emergency, special appeals ask for blankets and money for medicines which are sent to victims of famine or earthquakes.

You should be able to name some of the charities which collect money in this way.

3. Most of the aid sent to the developing world is in the form of BILATERAL AID. This is where one country sends aid directly to another.

Another major source of aid is sent through international organisations like the United Nations. This is MULTILATERAL AID. Aid is sent through United Nations organisations such as U.N.I.C.E.F., W.H.O. and U.N.E.S.C.O.. Find out what they stand for and what kind of aid they supply.

4. Much of the aid is spent on LARGE SCALE projects like airports and power stations.

5. Increasingly, aid is being given for SMALL SCALE, local projects such as BIOGAS plants or tree-planting schemes to reduce soil erosion. Many of these could be described as SELF-HELP schemes, as money is spent on small projects which local people become involved in.

6. Aid is also given in the form of food and medicines, particularly when drought, flooding or other natural disasters strike.

7. You should be able to describe examples of each of the types of aid described on page 36.
In addition, you should be able to describe the benefits which each brings as well as to explain why there may be problems. To help you, some of these are shown in the table below:

TYPE OF AID	ADVANTAGES	DISADVANTAGES
LARGE SCALE AID	- can assist many people - may employ many people - encourages long-term industrial development - source country makes money by supplying expertise and materials	- may be TIED to other agreements - often not cost-effective
SMALL SCALE AID (SELF HELP SCHEMES)	- many people benefit at local level - low-level technology which is easily understood - repair and maintenance is simple	- little benefit for source country
FOOD AND MEDICINE	- much needed improves health	- only useful in the long term if linked with training

8. It is argued, however, that not all aid is a good thing. Some of the problems include:

- not all aid may reach the people it is intended for
- it may destroy the local community: farmers may not continue to work if food is sent
- the wrong type of aid may be sent to an area
- local people may be put out of work, especially if 'experts' are sent in from abroad
- aid may only given if there is an agreement to supply spares or use materials from the source area
- much of the aid given to developing countries is military: planes, weapons, training. This does little to improve the standard of living.

18. ALLIANCES

1. Countries often join together into groups or ALLIANCES. They may do this for

- economic reasons
- political and military reasons

2. Economic reasons:
The European Community is a good example of an economic alliance. The countries which make up the E.C. have done this to make trading easier among themselves. Goods can pass from one country in the E.C. to another without having to pass through customs or pay taxes. Sometimes, countries which produce the same product, group together into another type of economic alliance. O.P.E.C. (The Organisation of Petroleum Exporting Countries) is an example. Most of the world's oil producers are members and they control the amount of oil exported, thus controlling its price.

3. Political and military reasons:
Countries often form alliances to defend themselves from possible attack. N.A.T.O. is one example, where the member countries share the responsibility for defence.

4. The existence of alliances, as well as their members is always changing. The recent changes in the Eastern European countries, which used to be communist members of the Warsaw Pact, show how quickly things can change.

You will not need to know details about any particular alliance, but should be aware of how

- certain alliances control large resources, affecting trade and development, and
- some alliances dominate international relations and exert a powerful influence on other countries' actions and borders.

19. TENSION AND CONFLICT

1. Certain areas of the world become scenes of TENSION and even CONFLICT.

2. Tension and conflict may be due to a number of causes. These include:

Civil unrest
Racial differences
Religious differences
Disputes over territory for historical reasons
Disputes over territory for economic or other reasons
Political differences
Disputes over areas of strategic importance

Sometimes more than one of these causes may be involved.

You should be able to name one example of present disputes in each of the categories above.

3. Be aware of the differences between local, national and international disputes.

4. Areas of conflict or tension are most likely to be of importance to the geographer when they involve more than one country.

5. This is especially true when the SUPERPOWERS are involved.

6. You should be able to describe the way in which superpowers have become involved in one area presently in conflict. This should focus on:

a) the effects on people living in the area
b) the way the superpowers influence the affected area
c) the dangers of potential ESCALATION into a war.

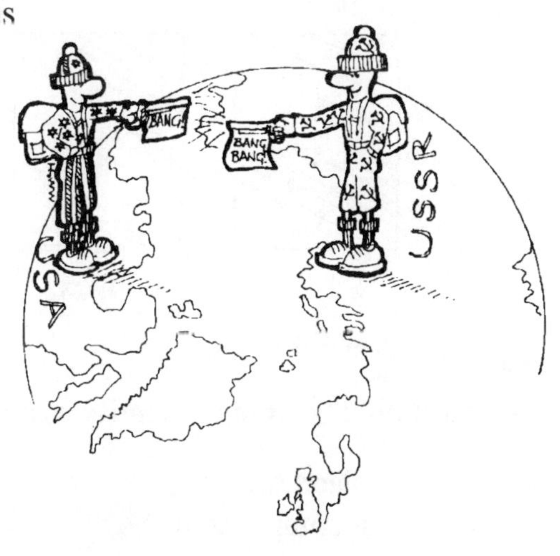

20. SKILLS

MAPPING SKILLS

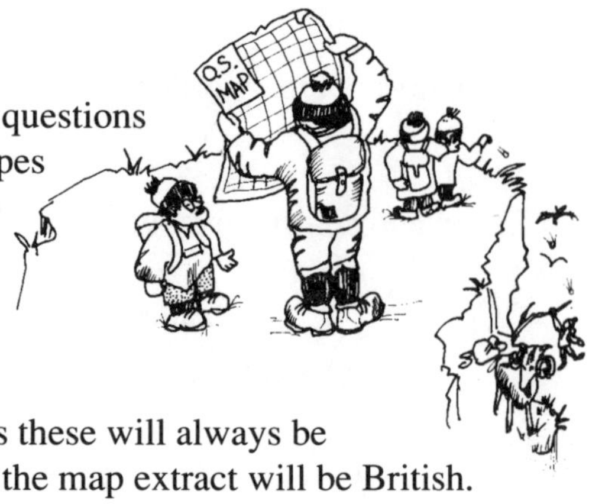

1. Papers at all three levels will contain a series of questions based on a map extract. Different scales and types of map can appear, although the most likely are Ordnance Survey 1:50 000 and 1:25 000 maps. Tourist maps (e.g. 1:250 000) are possible at Foundation Level.

   You will not have to memorise map symbols, as these will always be provided. There is no guarantee, however, that the map extract will be British.

2. You will be tested on your ability to use a number of mapping skills to extract information from the map, make deductions and identify a wide range of geographical features.

3. All this may sound rather daunting, but if you can do everything described on the next two pages, you have nothing to fear!

   It is essential to practise your mapping skills, so ask your teacher to set you questions on a sample map extract.

4. You will need to use grid references to locate places on any map. These will be 4 figure references at General and Foundation Level, *but you may have to use 6 figure references at Credit Level.*

   You may also be asked to use the scale of the map to calculate distances, and be able to describe locations in terms of direction (for example, "4 kilometres northeast of Stirling").

5. It is also important that you can use contour patterns to describe

   - slopes:

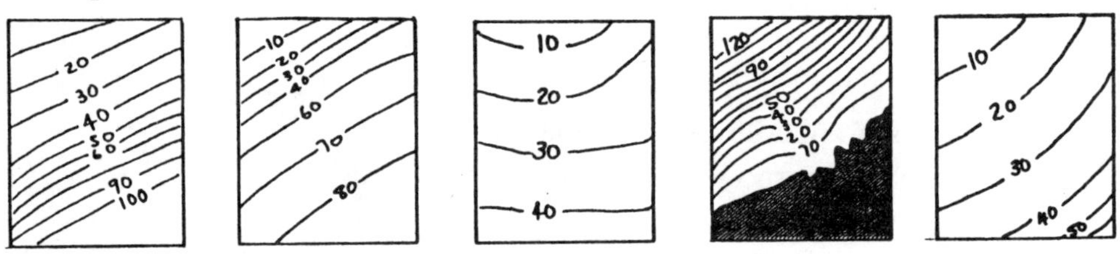

concave   convex   uniform   steep   gentle

   - landforms:

You should be able to identify a number of landforms, including:

upland area	lowland area
mountainous area	cliff
plateau	valley
ridge	col
pass	headland
scarp and dip slope	corrie

6. You may be faced with a cross section, on which you have to identify features from the map. This will look something like

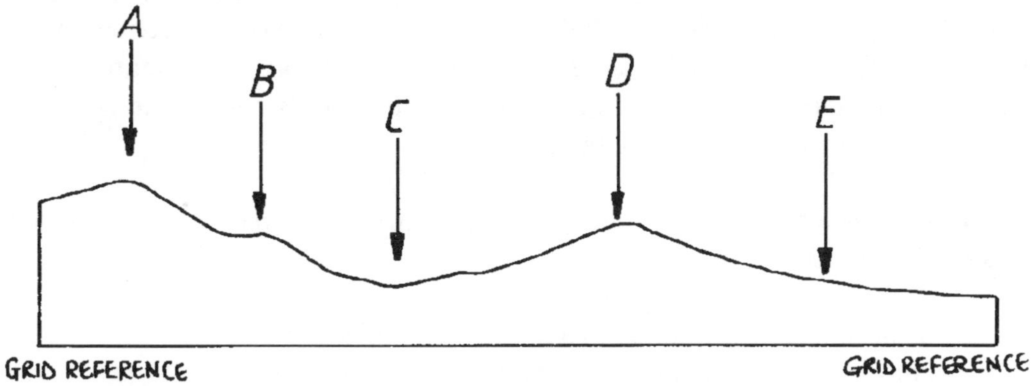

Normally you will be given a list of possible answers from which to select your answers. Practice makes this an easy exercise.

7. You will need to be able to identify different types of land use from the map. Here are some hints as to what to look for:

- stock farming (isolated settlements in an upland or poorly drained area)

- arable farming (isolated settlements in lowland or well drained areas)

- industrial areas (New industrial areas are often found at the edge of towns, with regular road patterns, whereas old industrial areas are normally found near town centres or rivers/canals. They often have irregular street patterns.)

- residential areas (old housing areas are found around the town centre, with closely packed streets, often at right angles. New housing areas are normally closer to the edge of the town, the most modern have gently curving street patterns, often following contour lines, with crescents and cul-de-sacs.)

- the Central Business District (or town centre) can usually be identified by the number of churches, public buildings, bus and rail stations, and converging roads.

The identification of different types of land use can be quite difficult, and requires practice. Why not buy a local O.S. map and look at areas you know well?

FORMS OF DATA EXTRACTION

1. Most of the questions you will answer in the exam are "resource based". This means you will be given a map, diagram, table, graph, sketch, photograph (or a combination of these) from which you will be able to extract information. It is essential to look carefully at all the data you are given. Nothing is there only for appearances: everything is of use in answering the question.

2. Sometimes you will required to change this information from one form into another. This might include

   - using statistics contained in a table to complete a graph
   - constructing a weather plot, given the relevant information
   - describing the characteristics of a population pyramid
   - measuring the distance between two places on a map
   - describing the course of a river on an Ordnance Survey map.

3. Sometimes you will have to extract data from a source. This might include

   - explaining the pattern of land use shown on a map of a farm
   - describing the trends shown in a graph or table
   - explaining why settlement growth in a map area has been restricted
   - explaining the distribution of steelworks in an area, given the appropriate information about raw materials, transport, markets, etc.

4. *Credit level questions are likely to have most sources of information. This means you will have to select the relevant information more carefully. The resources you are provided with in a Credit question are also likely to be more complex. Questions will be worth more marks, however, to compensate.*

ANSWERING KNOWLEDGE AND UNDERSTANDING QUESTIONS

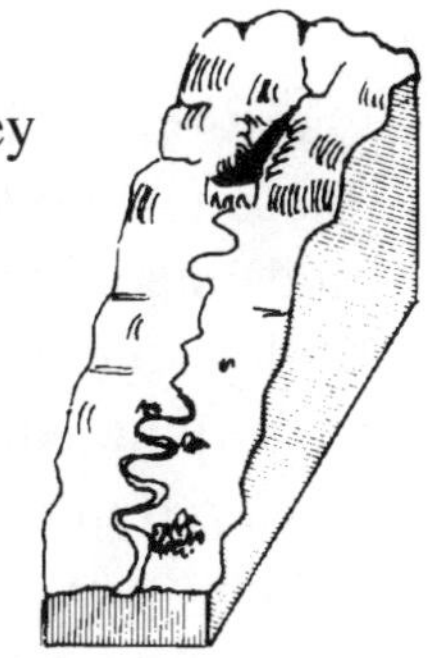

1. Questions testing knowledge are fairly straightforward to answer. They often require you to identify or select examples of geographical concepts.

The type of questions you might find include

- name three examples of features of glacial erosion from the O.S. map
- in which grid square would you find the C.B.D.?
- identify the river features shown in the block diagram
- describe the likely social and economic effects of the run-down of steelmaking in Lanarkshire
- describe the distribution of arable land in the map area.

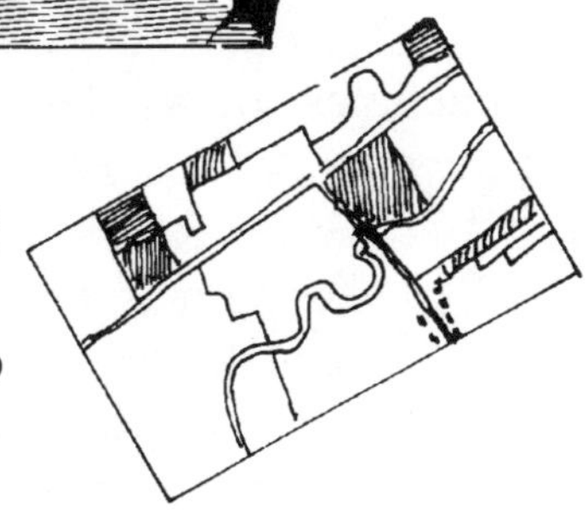

2. Questions testing understanding are rather more difficult. Not only must you be able to identify geographical concepts, you must be able to explain them.

You might be asked

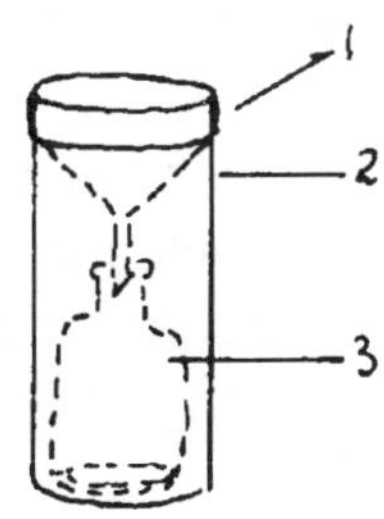

- explain, with the use of a diagram, how one of the features of glacial erosion in the sketch was formed
- explain why the city centre grew up in grid square 1234
- in what ways have the river features shown in the block diagram restricted the development of settlement beside the river?
- explain why traditional industries like steelmaking have declined over the last forty years
- explain the distribution of arable land in the map area.

3. Questions testing understanding are usually worth more marks than those testing knowledge.

4. As you can see, answering questions testing knowledge and understanding depends on the care and attention you have put into studying your notes. This book is designed to help you channel your study into the right areas. It cannot possibly hope to cover all the course content, but, used systematically with your class notes, it should ensure that you will be able to attempt every question with some hope of success.

HOW TO ANSWER EVALUATING QUESTIONS

1. Questions which test the skill of evaluating are rather different from those testing knowledge and understanding. They do require an understanding of the basic geographical elements, but it is your ability to make informed judgements which is most important. Answering these questions takes practice, and it is essential that you are aware of exactly what you are being asked to do. Evaluating questions will almost always provide you with sources of information which you have to examine before coming to conclusions.

2. Sometimes you will be asked to make a decision based on information received. For example:

   - using map evidence, describe the advantages and disadvantages of the site of Lanark
   - explain which of the types of foreign aid shown in the diagram would be of most benefit to Uganda
   - using the information given, do you think the Cruachan site was a suitable location for a hydroelectric power station?

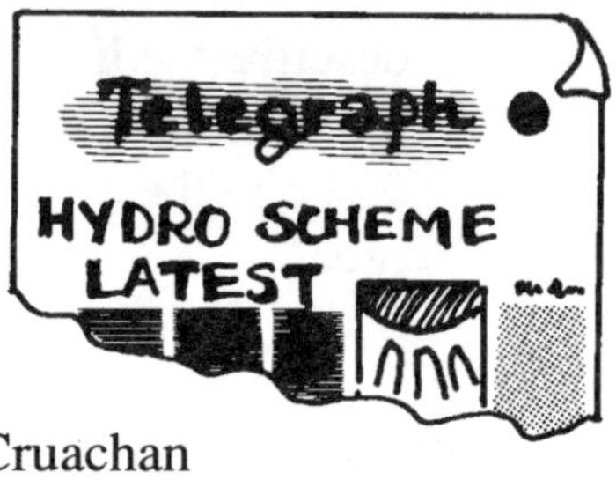

3. Sometimes you will be confronted with a number of points of view, and your task will be to support or reject each one. This requires careful handling: make sure all the points of view have been considered. In effect, you are being asked to examine both sides of an argument, and decide which is most suitable. For example:

   - the area shown on the map is to be made into an industrial estate. What are the advantages and disadvantages of this plan?
   - argue the case for and against the proposed quarry
   - explain how the development might bring benefits and problems to the area.

4. Another kind of question you may see is one where you have to identify bias or exaggeration. This is usually obvious in a cartoon or statement, where only one point of view is expressed. For example:

   - look at the statement from a Government official and state two ways in which he exaggerates his message
   - explain how the cartoon shows bias.

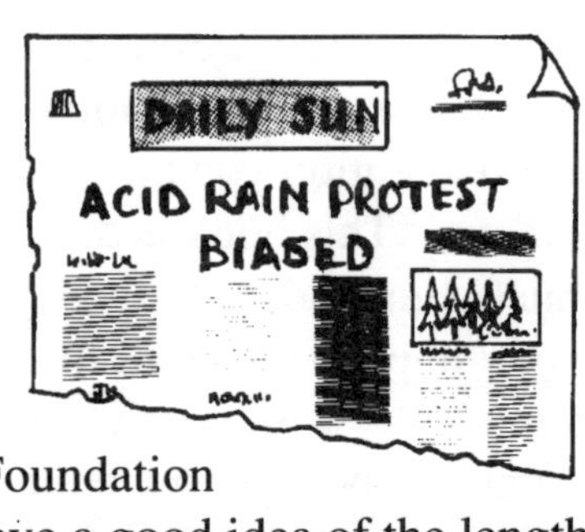

5. General questions are usually worth a maximum of 4 marks, and Foundation questions are seldom worth more than 2 marks each. In the General and Foundation Papers, you are given spaces to answer in, so you have a good idea of the length of answer which is expected. *Questions in the Credit Paper call for more extended answers, as you would expect. They are normally worth between 3 and 6 marks. In the Credit Paper, you will write your answers in an answer booklet, so try and match what you write to the marks available.* Don't write 20 lines for a 4 mark question!

21. INVESTIGATING

For many people, their geography Investigation is good news! The chance to work on a topic which interests them, in their own time, means that for many students, their top grade is awarded in the Investigation.

Your Investigation is assessed in four parts:

(a) PLANNING
(b) RESEARCHING AND SELECTING RELEVANT INFORMATION
(c) PROCESSING INFORMATION
(d) MAKING VALID CONCLUSIONS

HOW TO PLAN YOUR INVESTIGATION

1. Once you have decided on the subject of your Investigation (page 48) you will have to do some PLANNING. You can start by asking yourself some questlons:

- What do I want to find out? (What are my aims?)
- Where will I get my information?
- Is the project manageable? (too big a topic?)
- Is there enough scope to get a good award?

2. These questions (and answers) should go into your LOGBOOK. This is a very important part of the Investigation, as it will provide your teacher with evidence of what you have done.

Now is the time to get down to hard work! But first of all answer these questions in your logbook:

- Is it geography?
- Has my teacher given me the go-ahead?
- How will I allocate my time?
- Where do I start?

From now on, record everything you do in your logbook, including dates, information received, book or other references, observations, interviews, sketches or anything else of value.

3. Don't be afraid to ask for hclp. Be absolutely sure of what you are setting out to do: no-one drives off on holiday without knowing where he is going! So be sure you know the route you are taking and your final destination before you get under way!

HOW TO GATHER AND PROCESS INFORMATION

1. Where am I going to get my data?

   There are many sources of information, and the more of these you use the better the grade you will get for RESEARCH. Sources include:

TEXT........................	books, magazines, newspapers, libraries, posters
MAPS.......................	historical, geology, different scales, town plans, atlases, soil maps
DATA.......................	statistics, census reports, Scottish Office, library data bases, graphs
INTERVIEWS..........	friends, family, tourists, shoppers, librarians, questionnaires, on tape, on video
ILLUSTRATIONS...	photographs, sketches, cartoons, field sketches, diagrams
FIELD WORK..........	visits to streets, settlements, factories, rivers, coasts, and a million other things!

   Try to gather information from a number of these sources. Very often, the best Investigations involve actual field work rather than depending on library-based sources alone. Remember to keep in touch with your teacher!

2. Once you have gathered all the information you are likely to need, it has to be sifted. Not all can be used, and you must decide what is relevant to your Investigation. This can be done in your logbook too.

3. Now for PROCESSING. This means transforming a collection of data into a sensible Investigation.

   A pictureboard is a good idea here. On a sheet of paper, draw about 10 rectangles to represent the pages in your Investigation. On each page, describe very roughly what each final page will show. This will help you structure your work properly. Once you have done this, show it to your teacher. An example of a pictureboard is shown on this page. It doesn't have to be neat or accurate.
   Now put it into your logbook.

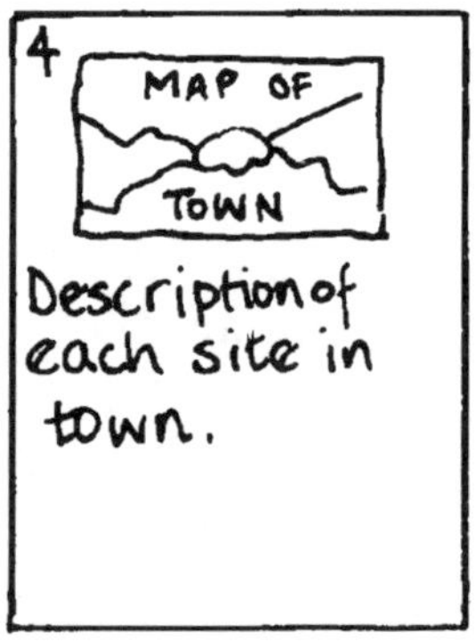

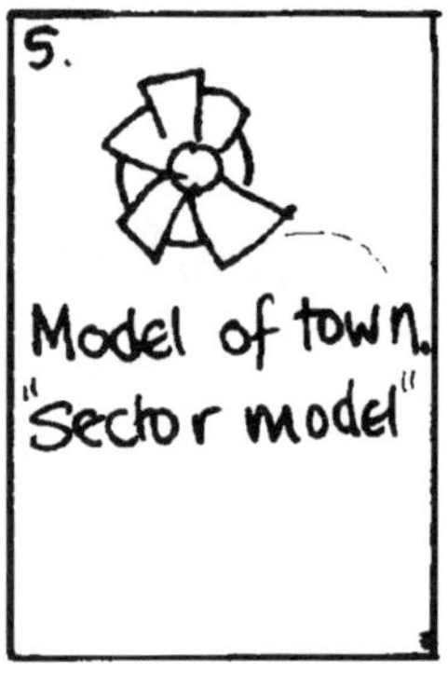

   The more ways you present your information, the better the grade you will get for processing.

   Use the rough draft contained in your pictureboards to write up your Investigation. Putting things into your own words is one form of processing. Others include compiling pie charts, line and bar graphs from data you have collected. Annotating photographs and sketches is a very valuable type of processing - it is possible to show a great deal of information without using much space. Wherever possible, try to draw your own maps, and make sure you include a key, scale and north point.

HOW TO PRESENT YOUR INVESTIGATION

1. Your final Investigation can be presented in a variety of forms. For example,

- a booklet of about 10 sides of A4 paper
- a poster or wall display
- a video programme, with accompanying notes
- a tape/slide programme.

However you decide to present your Investigation, you must check first with your teacher. And don't forget to include your logbook and picture-boards, as they might be required by the Exam Board.

2. MAKING VALID CONCLUSIONS is a very important part of your Investigation. You must draw the whole thing together, and show that you have answered the questions you set out in your aims. You should be able to answer these questions:

- have I done everything I set out to do?
- have I answered all my original questions?
- did I discover anything I didn't expect?
- if so, can I explain it?
- have I given reasons to explain what I found?
- is the whole Investigation clearly and logically expressed?
- have I discarded everything which doesn't answer the questions I asked?

3. Finally, note down all your references in a BIBLIOGRAPHY. This should include all books, magazines, TV programmes, map sources, etc.

Book references should include the author, title, publisher, year of publication, and chapter (or page), for example:

Jimmy Acne, "Geography for Spotty Adolescents", Blackhead Publishers, 1991, Chapter 4.

SUGGESTED TOPICS FOR YOUR INVESTIGATION

1. The only restriction facing you when you choose your Investigation topic is that it must relate to the KEY IDEAS in your geography course. These are briefly mentioned on page 4 of this book, but your teacher will give you a complete list.

2. The best Investigations include both FIELD WORK (surveying areas, asking questionnaires, taking photographs, making sketches) as well as INDOOR WORK (in the library, classroom, museum).

3. Some suggestions for your Investigation are:

- examine river, coastal or glacial features in your local area
- river pollution: where and why
- the effects of a drought or flood
- setting up a weather station and explain your findings
- comparing two local farms: why are they different?
- study a rural industry (e.g. fishing, fish farming, forestry)
- a land use conflict study in a rural landscape (e.g. conservation v. skiing in the Cairngorms)
- conservation of a valuable landscape (e.g. sand dunes)
- threats to fragile areas such as rainforest, oceans, the atmosphere, deserts
- changes in a settlement over time
- a study of urban problems
- a study of traffic congestion: causes and solutions
- comparing two spheres of influence
- why people shop in a certain area
- change in rural land use
- how an industry has changed over time
- comparing two industries
- reasons for industrial location: a comparison of two factories
- the effects on an area of an industry closing down
- the impact of a new bridge/ferry
- the effect of tourism in an area
- a comparison between two parks
- a study of a National Park
- a study of migration in an area
- the distribution of certain populations in an area
- a study of different energy sources
- an examination of local resources
- a study of diets in different areas
- how aid is spent in developing countries
- which type of foreign aid is best?
- the effects of war on an area
- pollution of the environment
- how soil erosion happens and its impact and solutions
- resource exploitation in difficult areas of the world
- the Greenhouse Effect: how can it be averted?

These are simply a number of possibilities. Whether you choose something from this list or something of your own, make sure you discuss it fully with your teacher before setting out on your Investigation. And good luck!